MANNERS
OUT AND ABOUT

JOSH PLATTNER

Consulting Editor, Diane Craig, M.A./Reading Specialist

Sandcastle

An Imprint of Abdo Publishing
abdopublishing.com

abdopublishing.com

Published by Abdo Publishing, a division of ABDO, PO Box 398166, Minneapolis, Minnesota 55439. Copyright © 2016 by Abdo Consulting Group, Inc. International copyrights reserved in all countries. No part of this book may be reproduced in any form without written permission from the publisher. SandCastle™ is a trademark and logo of Abdo Publishing.

Printed in the United States of America, North Mankato, Minnesota
062015
092015

THIS BOOK CONTAINS RECYCLED MATERIALS

Editor: Alex Kuskowski
Content Developer: Nancy Tuminelly
Cover and Interior Design and Production: Mighty Media, Inc.
Photo Credits: Shutterstock

Library of Congress Cataloging-in-Publication Data

Plattner, Josh, author.

Manners out and about / Josh Plattner ; consulting editor, Diane Craig, M.A./Reading Specialist.

pages cm. -- (Manners)

Audience: PreK to grade 3.

ISBN 978-1-62403-717-7

1. Courtesy--Juvenile literature. 2. Respect--Juvenile literature. 3. Etiquette for children and teenagers--Juvenile literature. I. Title.

BJ1533.C9P55 2016

395.1'22--dc23

2014046374

SandCastle™ Level: Transitional

SandCastle™ books are created by a team of professional educators, reading specialists, and content developers around five essential components—phonemic awareness, phonics, vocabulary, text comprehension, and fluency—to assist young readers as they develop reading skills and strategies and increase their general knowledge. All books are written, reviewed, and leveled for guided reading, early reading intervention, and Accelerated Reader™ programs for use in shared, guided, and independent reading and writing activities to support a balanced approach to literacy instruction. The SandCastle™ series has four levels that correspond to early literacy development. The levels are provided to help teachers and parents select appropriate books for young readers.

EMERGING · BEGINNING · **TRANSITIONAL** · FLUENT

CONTENTS

Manners Out and About   4

Care for Others   6

Perfect Pace   8

Hand Manners   10

Voice Control   12

Playing Politely   14

Fun with Others   16

Animal Actions   18

Considerate Concern   20

Keep It Up!   22

Glossary   24

MANNERS
OUT AND ABOUT

Good manners are great! They are important. Use them while you are out and about.

CARE FOR OTHERS

Have respect for others. Jen waits at the **crosswalk**. She watches where she is going.

PERFECT PACE

Dani and Steve run
in the park. They are
careful not to run into
other people.

HAND MANNERS

Keep your hands to
yourself. Don't point at
others. It is not **polite**.
Try a friendly wave.

VOICE CONTROL

Don't **disturb** others. Keep your voice at an **appropriate** level. Try not to yell.

PLAYING POLITELY

Take turns on the playground. Carrie loves to swing. She waited for her turn.

FUN WITH OTHERS

Be friendly in public.
You can make new
friends. Make sure
to smile!

ANIMAL ACTIONS

Animals can be friendly.
Matt knows to ask an adult
before petting a strange
animal. Be kind to the
animal. Be gentle too.

CONSIDERATE CONCERN

Stay away from fighting.
If you see a fight, tell an
adult. The adult will help.

KEEP IT UP!

Always practice good manners while you are out. Can you think of more? What else could you do?

GLOSSARY

appropriate – suitable, fitting, or proper for a specific occasion.

considerate – aware of the feelings and needs of others.

crosswalk – a specially marked path for people to walk safely across a street.

disturb – to bother or interrupt.

polite – having good manners or showing consideration for others.